Bucks County

A Photographic Celebration

Photography

Walter Choroszewski

Introduction

Governor Mark S. Schweiker

Published by

Aesthetic Press, Inc.

Somerville, New Jersey

Dedicated to the people of Bucks County

Bucks County
A Photographic Celebration

Edited and designed by Walter Choroszewski.
Printed in Korea - Second Printing 2002

ISBN 0-933605-10-2

Right - Schofield Ford

Covered Bridge,

Tyler State Park,

Newtown Township.

Overleaf - Stover-Myers Mill

County Park, Bedminster.

Aesthetic Press, Inc.
P.O. Box 5306, Somerville, NJ 08876-1303

Telephone: 908 369-3777
www.aestheticpress.com
e-mail: info@aestheticpress.com

Bucks County

As one of Pennsylvania's three original counties outlined by William Penn in 1682, Bucks County initially spanned from Philadelphia to the Kittatinny Mountains, almost seventy miles north and west of the city. It was named after Buckinghamshire, Penn's home in England, and he chose to make Bucks County his home in the New World.

Centuries later, in 1953, Bucks County became my home, too. My parents, John and Mary, themselves long-time Bucks County residents, raised six children here. It was here in a home blessed with family love and in the caring hands of community, that I was able to grow and prosper.

And for decades, I have seen Bucks County grow and prosper as well. From childhood to my high school days to my years in public service, I have seen Bucks County's population increase, its industries expand, and its culture diversify. But through all the change, one thing remains constant in Bucks County: its people, some of the most sincere, proud and determined people you will ever come to know. After all, that is our heritage.

In the 1630s the Swedes and Dutch were the first Europeans to settle in the Delaware Valley. England's claim to the land eventually led to its transfer to William Penn, a Quaker who encouraged emigration and whose treaty with the Lenape people established the new colony of Pennsylvania.

In the 1680s immigrants from England, Ireland, Wales, Holland and Germany continued to settle in the area. Penn stressed religious tolerance for all as the cultural make-up of the region diversified. He was a member of the Society of Friends and worshiped in Fallsington. Today, numerous churches, synagogues and houses of worship of many denominations remain in Bucks County—a testament to the success of Penn's experiment with freedom of worship.

Bucks County encompasses a large expanse of over six hundred square miles. It is located along the Delaware River, northeast of Philadelphia and ranges northwesterly towards the Lehigh Valley, with landforms that include Coastal Plain, Piedmont and the predominant rolling hills of the Triassic Lowlands.

With an identity all its own, the name "Bucks" conjures up impressions of a bucolic rolling countryside adorned with covered bridges, stone farmhouses and historic sites from the American Revolution through the Industrial Revolution. Bucks also brings to mind the scenic Delaware River and its companion Delaware Canal that meander beneath the rugged volcanic stone cliffs.

Bucks County not only inspires with its natural scenic beauty, but also appeals to each generation through the Arts: fine artists from Edward Hicks to the New Hope School artists, including Daniel Garber, Edward Redfield and Walter Elmer Schofield; literary masters like James Michener and Pearl S. Buck; musical and theater artists from Oscar Hammerstein II to the many performers who have taken the stage at the Bucks County Playhouse, including Robert Redford, Walter Matthau and Philadelphia's beloved Grace Kelly.

Henry Chapman Mercer, the Arts & Crafts pottery artist, archaeologist and passionate collector is another Bucks County icon. Three museums in Doylestown are dedicated to his treasures and creative genius. Bucks County has been home to innumerable other artists and craftsmen who have explored their creativity in this special place.

Walter Choroszewski is a photographic artist who has also been drawn to the beauty and magic of Bucks County. This Pennsylvania native has showcased the Mid-Atlantic for over twenty years and has published numerous regional books and calendars. I am pleased to collaborate with him on this latest production, **Bucks County, A Photographic Celebration.**

Since the mid-1980s Choroszewski has traversed the county capturing the very essence of Bucks, with his cameras, in preparation for this book. He presents the familiar, yet offers us a new perspective. His love of nature, respect for history and his celebration of life is evident throughout these pages—he has found fertile ground in Bucks County.

Choroszewski takes us on natural journeys—to a moody sunrise on Aquetong Lake, to a fresh snowfall blanketing Ringing Rocks, to Lumberville where an October mist rises from the river. A curious goat greets him at the Thompson-Neely farm; a family of Canada geese marches along the Delaware in Taylorsville and a colorful rooster shines in the sun at Cuttalossa Farm.

He revels in the local architecture: the classic Greek columns at Andalusia, brick-lined portals of a stone barn in Riegelsville, the star accent on Durham Mill and classic covered bridges from the Neshaminy Creek to Cabin Run. Bucks history is revealed in Choroszewski's images of the Parry Mansion, Octagonal School House and Liberty Hall; and the American Revolution is commemorated with photographs of Washington Crossing Historic Park, Summerseat and the David Library of The American Revolution.

Walter Choroszewski also enjoys meeting the people of Bucks, as he attends the varied events and festivals that celebrate life in the county. He introduces us to Bucks County's TV personality and restaurateur, Chef Tell Erhardt, and to renowned watercolor artist, Ranulph Bye, whose Bucks County paintings are familiar to many. He captures delight in the face of a child as she rides the Grand Carousel at Lahaska, pride in a costumed dancer at the Pearl S. Buck International Day Festival, and patriotism of parade onlookers in Sellersville.

Through Choroszewski's pictures, so many memories have been brought to mind of my times in Bucks County, like family walks through Washington Crossing or quiet dinners in picturesque New Hope. Pennsbury Manor, William Penn's summer home, remains a personal favorite, emanating grace and the ideals of Bucks' people in its architecture and style.

The James A. Michener Art Museum—housed in the renovated 1884 Bucks County Prison in Doylestown, and showcasing one of the finest collections of Pennsylvania art and sculpture—is another of my favorite destinations. I have enjoyed these county landmarks that offer wholesome and enjoyable experiences for residents and visitors alike; all brought to life by Walter Choroszewski in the pages that follow.

In a moment's reflection, I ponder a Bucks County that steered my life's journey. From the earliest years, Bucks County's people and nature have guided me along a path that promotes community and civic involvement. That ideal, no doubt, propelled my first run for public office in Middletown, civic contributions as both a township supervisor and Bucks County Commissioner. As the former Lieutenant Governor, and now as Governor, I continue to emphasize stronger communities throughout our Commonwealth.

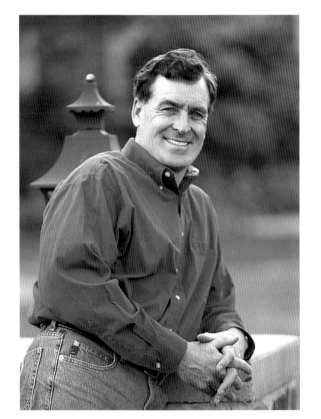

As we begin the 21st Century, Pennsylvania enjoys unprecedented levels of economic, social and community building success. Just as it did 300 years ago, Bucks County today is at the forefront, boldly leading the way to a more prosperous tomorrow while nurturing and even building on its historic past. It is all part of the Bucks County experience—an experience I have proudly lived and touted, time and time again, to many across this Commonwealth, our nation and world.

Yes, Bucks County's rich history is something to be cherished and shared with generations to come. For this reason, I invite you to view these photographs that bring the essence of Bucks County into your heart and home.

Mark Schweiker

Mark S. Schweiker
Governor
Commonwealth of Pennsylvania

Above - Display, Burgess Foulke House, Quakertown.

Left - Fallsington Days, Fallsington.

Parry Mansion, New Hope.

Above - Richardson House, Langhorne.

Right - Historic district, Water Street, Hulmeville.

Above - 300th Anniversary Celebration, Buckingham.

Left - Horse & carriage ride, New Hope.

Mules on canal towpath, New Hope.

Above - Historic Borough Council Chamber, Newtown.

Opposite - General Store and Post Office, Carversville.

Above - Pigeon atop Historic Association Library, Langhorne.

Right - Detail, Ferry Street, New Hope.

Opposite - Frank Arena's sculpture,

"Washington Crossing The Delaware," Upper Makefield.

17

Phillips Mill Art Center,

Solebury.

Above - Detail,
art gallery, New Hope.

Above Right - Artist's
table, Carversville.

Right - Renowned
watercolor artist,
Ranulph Bye,
Mechanicsville.

Above - Sunset, National Shrine of Our Lady of Czestochowa, New Britain.

Opposite - Bucks County places of worship.

Saint Katharine Drexel Shrine, Bensalem

Durham Union Church, Durham

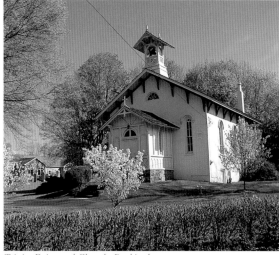

Trinity Episcopal Church, Buckingham

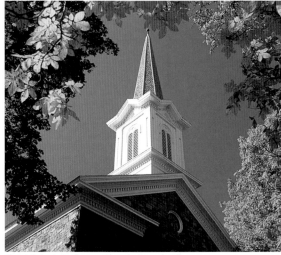

Saint Peter's Lutheran Church, Riegelsville

Rock Ridge Chapel, Wismer

Temple Shalom, Levittown

Trinity United Church of Christ, Telford

Christ The King Church, Tullytown

St. Luke's United Church of Christ, Dublin

Above - Crossing the dam,

Tyler State Park, Newtown.

Left - Goslings, Upper Makefield.

22

Above - Canada Goose family,

Washington Crossing Historic Park.

Right - Mallard ducks, Lake Afton, Yardley.

Above - Delaware Canal, New Hope.

Delaware River and Delaware Canal, Lumberville.

Above - Perkasie Carousel,
Perkasie.

Right - Pony rides, A-Day,
Delaware Valley College,
Doylestown Township.

Opposite - Grand Carousel,
Peddler's Village, Lahaska.

Above - Burgess Lea Barn, Solebury.

Opposite - Barn, Springfield.

Overleaf - Balloon festival, Milford.

Above - Churchville Nature Center, Northampton.

Left - Five Mile Woods Nature Preserve, Lower Makefield.

Above - Tamenend Nature Center, Upper Southampton.

Right - Silver Lake Nature Center, Bristol Township.

Above - Car Show, Bristol.

Top Left - MG Car Show, Doylestown.

Opposite - New Hope Automobile Show, New Hope.

Left - Garden photographer
and writer, Derek Fell, with
his Shetland Sheepdog,
"Rex," Tinicum.
Opposite - Burpee display
gardens, Fordhook Farm,
Doylestown Township.

36

Sailing, Lake Nockamixon,

Nockamixon State Park, Haycock.

Steeple of St. Matthew's

Lutheran Church, Bedminster.

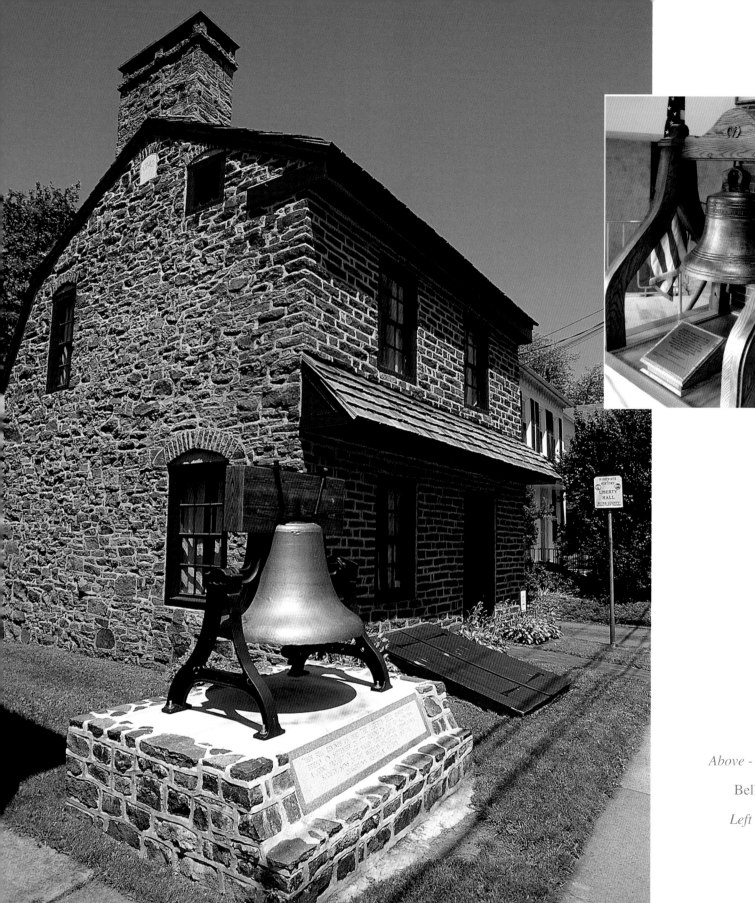

Above - Bucks County
Bell, Doylestown.
Left - Liberty Hall,
Quakertown.

Above - Flags and porches, Pleasant Valley.

Right - Pansies, Peddler's Village, Lahaska.

41

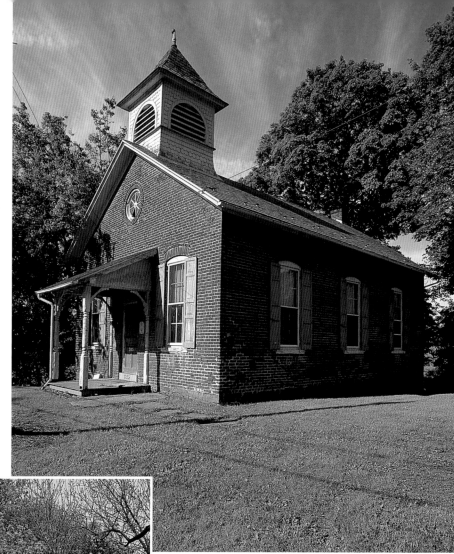

Early school buildings:

Above - Springfield School, Springfield.

Top Left - Old Warrington School, Warrington.

Left - Octagonal School, Wrightstown.

Above - Shelly School, Richland.

Right - Colonial reenactors,

Washington Crossing Historic Park,

Upper Makefield.

Above - Trenton-Morrisville Bridge, Morrisville.

Right - Wheat, Milford.

Opposite - Kite Day, Core Creek State Park, Middletown.

Memorial Day Parades:

This page - Sellersville.

Opposite, Top - Warminster.

Opposite, Bottom - Perkasie.

Covered Bridges:

Above - Pine Valley Bridge, New Britain.

Top - Uhlerstown Bridge, Tinicum.

Left - Cabin Run Bridge, Plumstead.

Opposite - Loux Bridge, Plumstead.

A-Day, Delaware Valley College, Doylestown.

Grange Fair, Wrightstown:

Above - Tractor display.

Right - 4-H Sheep Club.

51

Yellow Goat's Beard

Columbine

Water Hyacinth

Fleabane

Water Hemlock

Flame Azalea

Fire Pink

Eastern Lupine

St. John's Wort

Above - Barn detail, Riegelsville.

Opposite - Wildflowers, Bowman's Hill Wildflower Preserve, Solebury.

Overleaf - Nockamixon Dam, Tohickon Creek, Bedminster.

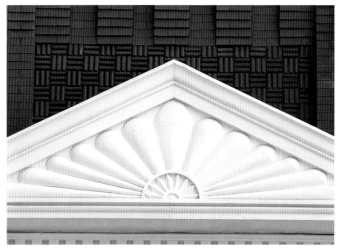

Architectural details,

Historic District, Doylestown.

Opposite - Mercer Museum, Doylestown.

Above - The Red Barn, Peddler's Village, Lahaska.

Left - Richland Auction Hall, Richland.

58

Above - Antiques Show, Stover County Park, Tinicum.

Right - Rice's Market, Solebury.

59

Thompson-Neely House, Solebury.

60

Above - Historic 1769
Old Presbyterian Church,
Newtown.

Right - Peter Taylor Farmstead,
Newtown Township.

Votive candles,
National Shrine of
Our Lady of Czestochowa,
New Britain Township.

Above - Tall ship,
"Gazela Phildadelphia,"
visiting port of Bristol.
Right - Newtown Hardware
House, Newtown Borough.

Above - Cuttalossa Farm, Solebury.

Left - Star detail, Durham Mill, Durham.

Opposite - Stone barn, Springfield.

Above - Musicians,

Fall State Craft Festival,

Tyler State Park.

Left - Folk Festival,

Mercer Museum, Doylestown.

Railroad bridge,

Delaware River, Lower Makefield.

Stone arch bridges:

Above - Eight arch bridge,

Dark Hollow Park, Warwick.

Left - Double arch bridge,

Cooks Creek, Durham.

Top Left - Railroad bridge,

Playwicki County Park, Middletown.

69

Above - Mt. Gilead A.M.E. Church,
Underground Railroad site, Buckingham.
Left- Mount Olive Cemetery, Langhorne.

Above - Bethlehem A.M.E. Church,

Underground Railroad site, Langhorne.

Right - Reverend Roselin Martin with

Black Historian, Walter Jacobs, Langhorne.

71

Above - Curious goat, Thompson-Neely Farm, Solebury.

Opposite - Curious cats on a fence, Wrightstown.

72

Above - Riegelsville
Public Library, Riegelsville.
Left - The Old Library by
Lake Afton, Yardley.
Right - Morrisville
Public Library, Morrisville.

Village Library, Wrightstown.

Smithtown Creek,

Tinicum.

Above - Trees along Afton Lake, Yardley.

Right - Forest detail, Ringing Rocks County Park, Bridgeton.

Above - Farm, Nockamixon.

Top - Hay time, East Rockhill.

Right - Hay time, Hilltown.

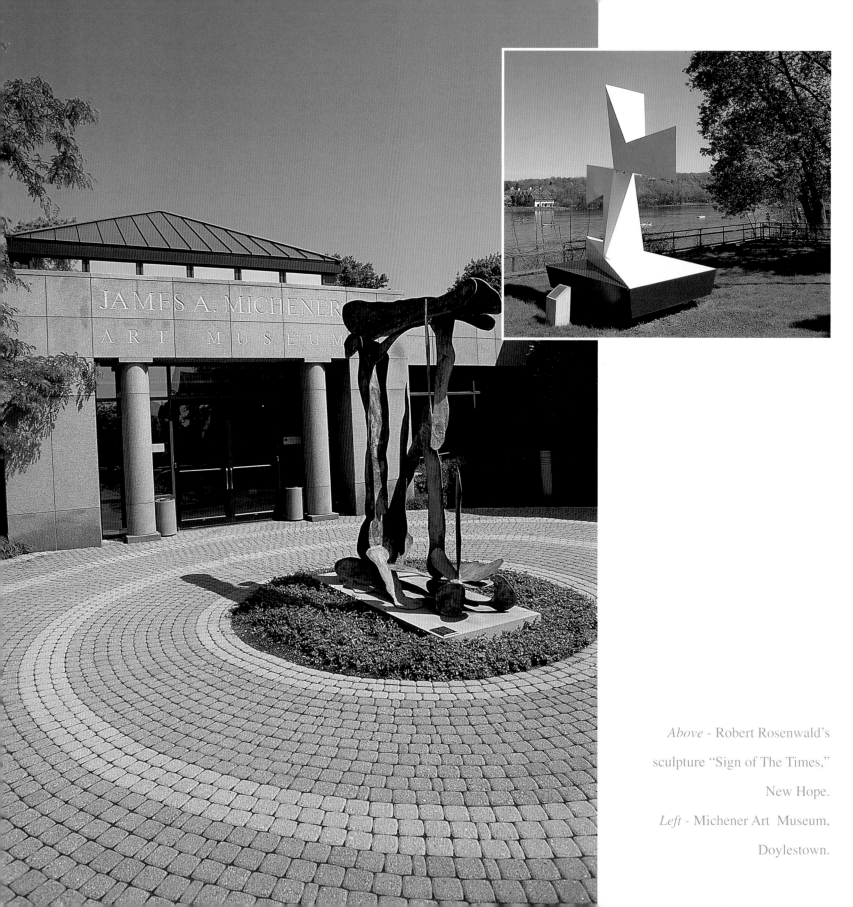

Above - Robert Rosenwald's
sculpture "Sign of The Times,"
New Hope.
Left - Michener Art Museum,
Doylestown.

Above - Kinsman Company,
Point Pleasant.
Left - Bucks County
Community College,
Newtown Township.

81

Above - Ringing Rocks County Park, Bridgeton.

Right - High Rocks State Park, Tinicum.

Chef Tell Erhardt,
The Manor House,
Upper Black Eddy.

Above - King George II Inn, Bristol.

Top - Richlandtown Inn, Richlandtown.

Left - Dilly's Corner, Center Bridge.

IN PLANNING NEWTOWN
WILLIAM PENN RESERVED ABOUT
THIRTY ACRES OF LAND AS A COMMON
BORDERING ON NEWTOWN CREEK
GIVING FREE USE OF WATER AND PASTURE TO ALL
OF THAT GRANT THIS ONE LOT REMAINS
AS PUBLIC PROPERTY

Above - Historic Fallsington, Falls Township.

Left - Historic marker, Newtown.

Mueller Display Gardens, Solebury.

Scenes from polo matches,

Bucks County Horse Park,

Revere, Nockamixon.

Above- Cuttalossa Creek, Solebury.

Right - Falls Creek, Bridgeton.

90

Above - Puerto Rican
Day Festival, Bristol.
Left - Pennsylvania
State Fair, Bensalem.

Peddler's Village, Lahaska.

Pearl S. Buck House, Hilltown.

Bucks County
Designer Show Houses,
Doylestown Township.

Above - Summerseat,

Washington's Headquarters, Morrisville.

Top Left- Durham boat,

Washington Crossing Historic Park.

Left - McConkey's Ferry Inn,

Washington Crossing Historic Park.

Above - Moland House, Washington's Headquarters, Warwick.

Top - Ceremony at soldiers graves, Washington Crossing Historic Park.

Right - David Library of the American Revolution,

Upper Makefield.

Above - Honey Hollow Audubon Center, Solebury.

Right - Sign, Bird In Hand Inn, Newtown.

Opposite - Birdhouses, Durham Furnace.

BIRD IN HAND

Above - Garden detail, Carversville.

Opposite - Dancers at Pearl S. Buck International Day Festival, Hilltown.

Overleaf - Dawn on Aquetong Lake, Solebury.

Above - Delaware
River, Bristol.
Left - Lake
Nockamixon,
Haycock.

Above - Penn Warner Club,
Scotts Creek, Falls Township.
Right - Tohickon launch ramp,
Lake Nockamixon State Park,
East Rockhill.

Left - View from
Bowman's Tower,
Upper Makefield.
Opposite - Colonial yarn,
Washington Crossing
Historic Park.
Opposite Top - Rooster,
Solebury.

Bucks County Fire Companies:

Above - Antique Truck, Chalfont.

Top Right - Truck, Warminster.

Top Left - Fire Station, Silverdale.

Left - Truck, Haycock.

Far Left - Sign, Midway, Buckingham.

Volunteer firefighters, Trumbauersville.

TO THE MEMORY OF THE LENNI LENAPE INDIANS
ANCIENT OWNERS OF THIS REGION
THESE STONES ARE PLACED AT THIS SPOT
THE STARTING POINT OF THE
INDIAN WALK
SEPTEMBER 19, 1737.
BUCS. CO. HIST. SOC. 1890

Above - Turtle, Bristol Township.

Top - Playwicky Indian Town monument, Lower Southampton.

Left - Walking Purchase monument, Wrightstown.

Opposite - Detail, Moravian Pottery & Tile Works, Doylestown.

Right - Tubing at
Sesame Place, Middletown.
Opposite Top - Tubing on
the Delaware River, near
Point Pleasant, Plumstead.
Opposite Bottom - Water
play at Ralph Stover State
Park, Plumstead.

113

Above - Fairways Golf &
Country Club, Warrington.
Top - Northampton Valley
Golf & Country Club, Richboro.
Right - Aerial,
Yardley Country Club, Yardley.

Above - Sign, Bucks County Historical Society, Doylestown.

Right - Signs & markers of Bucks County.

Penndel

Springfield

Yardley

Bedminster

Plumstead

Morrisville

Doylestown Township

Newtown Township

Solebury

Bristol Township

Churchville

Above - Statue, William Penn,

Pennsbury Manor,

Falls Township.

Top - Friends Meeting

House, Buckingham.

Left - Friends Meeting

House, Solebury.

Above - Friends Meeting House, Newtown.

Left - Friends Meeting House, Wrightstown.

Above - Delaware Valley College,

Doylestown Township.

Right - Philadelphia Biblical University,

Langhorne Manor.

Tyler Hall,

Bucks County

Community College,

Newtown Township.

New Hope & Ivyland Railroad:

Above - New Hope.

Left - Buckingham.

Above - Amtrak train, Cornwells Heights.

Right - Window, Perkasie Historical Society, Perkasie.

Above - Fonthill Museum, Doylestown.

Opposite - Andalusia, Bensalem.

Horses:

Above - Durham.

Left - Solebury.

Right - West Rockhill.

Above - Ravenhead Bed & Breakfast, Hartsville.

Left - Bridgetown Mill House, Langhorne.

Opposite Top - Beyond The Sea Bed & Breakfast, Ivyland.

Opposite Bottom - EverMay On-The-Delaware, Erwinna.

Overleaf-I - Morning fog, Delaware River, Solebury.

Overleaf-II - Pennsbury Manor, Falls.

Epilogue

The October air was crisp, the morning light was clear and a soft blue mist danced lightly over the mirrored surface of the Neshaminy Creek. Above, spanned the 19th century Schofield Ford Covered Bridge with autumn leaves shining like gold surrounding its silvery boards and diamond windows—I knew I had captured a special moment.

The year was 1986 and I was actively shooting the Bucks County countryside for what I thought would be my second photographic book project. Instead, the detours of life put this project "on hold" for 15 years. During that hiatus, the original Schofield Ford Covered Bridge, which I had photographed for the cover, met its untimely end to arson in 1991.

I had returned many times and continued my photography of Bucks County through the 1990s as the book project lived on in my heart. During those years, the people of Newtown and Bucks County also had a passion for their lost historic bridge and successfully reconstructed and dedicated the Schofield Ford Covered Bridge in 1997.

As the new millennium approached I was actively producing many regional projects and the time seemed right to revitalize the Bucks County book project. Through 2000 my photography of the county increased and was completed in early 2001. I felt honored when Lieutenant Governor Mark S. Schweiker offered to write an introduction for **Bucks County, A Photographic Celebration**—*my tenth book.*

Although I have lived in New Jersey for many years, I still consider Pennsylvania to be my home, as I was born and raised in the anthracite coal region of Northeastern Pennsylvania and graduated from Penn State University in 1975. It was during my college years that I made my first visit to Bucks County, traveling along the scenic Route 611 from the Pocono Mountains to Philadelphia.

I didn't return to the county until the mid-1980s when I was considering it as a new location for our family home. It was during those house hunting sojourns that I fell in love with the natural beauty, rich history and many artistic treasures of Bucks County.

I have traveled throughout this very large county—often confused by the northwest- southeast orientation of its roads. I have discovered the subtle facets of three distinctive regions of Upper, Central and Lower Bucks County. These regions are each unique with differences based on land types, economy, as well as the ethnicity of their first settlers. As an outside observer, I see Bucks County as a single entity, and I have included a photo from every municipality in this book.

Upper Bucks offers a rural small-town charm with rugged natural beauty that reminds me of my home in Northeastern Pennsylvania. Central Bucks is blessed with quaint villages and classic farms across its rolling hills and is rich in culture and the arts. Lower Bucks has a suburban energy emanating from nearby Philadelphia, and interspersed with a proud history dating back to William Penn. However, it is the spectacular Delaware River, shared by all regions, that welcomes me with each crossing and links my travels through North, Central and South.

During the years of this project I have made many new friends in Bucks County who warmly welcomed my visits and enthusiastically helped me in my quest for images.

I wish to thank Governor Mark S. Schweiker for his thoughtful words, but moreover, for being a new friend in Pennsylvania.

Walter Choroszewski